Pilipino
phrasebook

lonely planet

John U Wolff

Pilipino Phrasebook

Published by
  Lonely Planet Publications
  Head Office: PO Box 617, Hawthorn, Vic 3122, Australia
  Branches: 155 Filbert St, Suite 251, Oakland, CA 94607, USA
                    10 Barley Mow Passage, Chiswick, London W4 4PH, UK
                    71 bis rue du Cardinal Lemoine, 75005 Paris, France

Printed by
  Colorcraft, Hong Kong

First published
September 1988

Editor	Mark Balla
Cover design & illustrations	Greg Herriman
Typesetting & design	Ann Jeffree

National Library of Australia Cataloguing in Publication Data

Wolff, John U
  Pilipino Phrasebook

  ISBN 0 86442 064 1

  1. Pilipino Language – Conversation and phrase books – English. I. Title.
  (Series: Language survival kit).

499.211'834'21
© Copyright Lonely Planet, 1988

Contents

Introduction

Pilipino, or Tagalog as it is also known, is one of the two official languages of the Philippines. The other is English. Although English is the medium of education above the primary level and is widely spoken at least to some extent by much of the population, almost everyone under 60 speaks Pilipino, even in areas where it is not the native language.

Pilipino is the language which Filipinos use among themselves. People tend to feel more at home with Pilipino, whereas English feels stilted and artificial. To communicate on a personal level one must use Pilipino, though it may often be mixed with English. Foreigners who try speaking Pilipino invariably meet with great approval from the people and will often find Pilipino to be the only way to make real contact.

Pilipino is a member of the Austronesian or Malayo-Polynesian language family, which includes all of the languages of insular South-East Asia (Indonesia and the Philippines) including the tribal languages of Taiwan, some of the mainland South-East Asian languages, and most of the languages of New Guinea and Oceania. Pilipino is one of around 100 languages spoken in the Philippines and was originally spoken in the Manila area and in the provinces surrounding Manila Bay. Tagalog has been an official language of the Philippines since the end of 1937, and since the early '60s it has been known in popular parlance as Pilipino.

Pilipino has spread widely throughout the Philippines in the past 50 years, both because of official government policy mandating its study in schools, and because of the economic and social importance of the Manila area and because of the influence of Pilipino mass-media, films, broadcasts, and, to some extent, reading materials, which have a wide audience throughout the country. Further, in many areas where migration patterns have led to populations with a great deal of ethnic and linguistic diversity, Pilipino has become the primary means of intergroup communication. Thus Pilipino is now the main language not only in its home base but in some of the major cities of Palawan and Mindanao and has become the second language everywhere except in the most isolated regions.

Pronunciation

Vowels

Pilipino pronunciation offers few complications for English speakers. There are five vowels: **i, e, a, o, u**, and four diphthongs: **ay, oy, iw, aw**. The following list gives an approximate pronunciation.

i – similar to English 'ee' in meet
bili – buy

e – similar to English 'e' in let
empényo – request

a – similar to English 'a' in father
bála – bullet

o – similar to English 'o' in God
óras – time

u – similar to English 'oo' in too
úna – first, foremost

Diphthongs

ay – similar to English 'igh' in high
báhay – house

Normally this diphthong occurs only at the end of the word. Orthographic **ay** anywhere other than at the end of the word and in monosyllables is pronounced like **e**.

kay (pronounced *ke*) – to
pára kay (ke) john – for John

oy (sometimes **uy**) – similar to English 'oi' in boil
apoy (apuy) – fire

iw – a sound beginning with 'ee' and moving to 'oo',
similar to English 'ew' in few.
bitiw – release

aw – similar to English 'ou' in house
ikaw – you

Vowels in sequence
If several vowels are written in a sequence, each is
pronounced distinctly, separated by a glottal stop. A glottal
stop is the 'sound' that replaces 'tt' in 'bottle' when said by a
cockney. It also occurs in the middle of 'oh-oh!'.
táo (ta-o) – man
mabait (maba-it) – well-behaved

Vowels can be long or short. Normally, length is not
indicated in Pilipino orthography. In this book, length is
indicated by an acute accent.
makákisáma – be sociable
makákáin – edible
pagkakáiba – difference
nakákabili – can buy
mákatulog – fall asleep
makatúlog – can sleep

Consonants

Most consonants in Pilipino are pronounced in much the same way as are their English counterparts. There are, however, a few which warrant a mention, as they often cause difficulties for English speakers.

Aspiration

Aspiration does occur in the English language, but it is not important in determining the meaning of any words. For this reason it is effectively redundant. This leads to the problem that many English speakers cannot hear the difference between aspirated and unaspirated consonants. Basically aspiration is a puff of air which follows a consonant. If you say 'star' and 'tar', 'ski' and 'key', and 'spy' and 'pie' with your hand in front of your mouth, you will notice that the breath is much more forceful when 't', 'k' and 'p' are at the beginning of the word. This is aspiration. Quite simply, Pilipino does not have aspiration, even at the beginning of a word.

Glottal stop

As mentioned in the section on vowels, when there is a sequence of vowels they are separated by glottal stops.

The glottal stop only occurs before a pause. In the middle of a phrase it is dropped, and the vowel preceding is lengthened.

walà	there is none
walá na	they're all gone
mámayà	later
mámayá na	make it another time

Other difficult consonants

There is really only one consonant in Pilipino which most English speakers do not use every day – r. Its pronunciation is the same as in Spanish. It is like a rolled 'r', but the tongue only taps against the roof of the mouth once.

Finally there is the consonant **ng**. This is the same as in the English word 'sing'. The only difference is that it can occur anywhere in a word – beginning, middle, or end. All English speakers can make this sound, otherwise they wouldn't be able to say 'sing', and yet many people have difficulty in putting it at the beginning of a word. If it is any consolation, this is only a mental block.

Stress

Stress is automatically on the last long vowel in the word. If the word contains no long vowels, stress is on the final syllable. The stressed syllable is highlighted in the following examples:

mánunulat	writer
nagwáwalang-bahálà	not care
nagbábasa	be reading
pagbabasa	a reading
kumakáin	be eating

Spelling Conventions

The spelling tells us unequivocally how a Pilipino word is pronounced except that vowel length and glottal stops (here indicated by acute (ŕ) and grave (ɩ) accents respectively) are not indicated. Further the particle *nang* (discussed in the grammar section) is written *ng* with spaces on both sides and the plural particle *manga* is written *mga*.

Grammar

Pilipino is a complicated language. In this section you will find some rules which may or may not be passed over.

Content words in Pilipino tend to be long and consist of roots plus one or several affixes. Pilipino conjugation and word formation is far too complex to handle here, even in its general outlines, but the syntax – how words go together in a sentence, is fairly straight forward. The affixed words (ie those words with prefixes, suffixes and 'infixes') are fairly free to be plugged in anywhere in the sentence, so that if you have some notion of the syntax and learn affixed forms as vocabulary items, you can form numerous new sentences.

Word Order

In Pilipino declarative sentences (not questions) the word or phrase which expresses the main point being made is most often the first word in the sentence. In the following sentence the main point being made relates to the size of 'his house' – *malaki* (big). The thing about which the point is being made is generally placed second in the sentence, although there are exceptions (to be discussed later).

His house is big.
    malaki ang báhay niya (literally 'big the house of him')

The same pattern can be seen in the following sentences. The major difficulty with Pilipino word order for an English speaker is determining what the main point is. Practice makes perfect!

My name is John.
  john ang pangálan ko (literally 'John the name of me')
John is coming now.
  dumárating na si john (literally 'is coming now John')
My teacher is coming now.
  dumárating na ang títser ko (literally 'is coming now my
  teacher')
The children are in Manila.
  násа mayníla ang mga bátà (literally 'are at Manila the
  children')

Questions

In Pilipino, statements and questions follow the same word
order.

Where are they?
  násaan sila? (literally 'are where they?')
Are they coming now?
  dumárating na ba sila? (literally 'coming now they?')

Question words
where
  saan
who
  sino
how
  paano
how many
  ilan
why
  bákit

where is
  násaan
what
  ano
when
  kailan
how much
  magkáno
which (of several)
  alin

For questions which do not have a question word the particle *ba* is used. It is placed in the second position in the sentence, and plays the same role as a question mark in English.

Is John in Manila?
  nása maynílá ba si john?

Word Order Exceptions

The negative marker *hindí* is placed first in the sentence.
The house is not big.
  hindí malaki ang báhay (literally 'not big the house')

Words of two syllables or less come immediately after the first word in the sentence. The two following examples exemplify this rule (notice the position of *ba* in both).

Is their house big?
  malaki ba ang báhay nila?
Isn't their house big?
  hindí ba malaki ang báhay nila?

For emphasis it is possible to begin a sentence with the subject, but for everyday speech this is not likely to be of particular importance.

Verbs

Verbs are conjugated in Pilipino, that is, they express tense and many other things which have to be expressed by phrases in English. However, the same verb is used for all persons.

I am asleep.
  natútúlog ako
You are asleep.
  natútúlog ka
He is asleep.
  natútúlog siya
John is asleep.
  natútúlog si john
The children are asleep.
  natútúlog ang mga bátà

But the verb is changed for tense:

I fell asleep.
  nákatulog ako
I will go to sleep.
  matútúlog ako

The Pilipino verb can express things which in English must be expressed with a phrase.

I was sleeping on my job.
  tinútulúgan ko ang trabáho ko
I put the child to sleep.
  pinatúlog ko ang bátà

Since verb conjugation is complicated, beginners should learn each verb form as an individual vocabulary item.

Nouns
Pilipino nouns are not inflected (changed for number or case). The plural is formed by placing the particle *mga* (pronounced *manga*) directly before the pluralised noun:

book	*libro*
books	*mga libro*

Names (of people and places) are preceded by *si*, *ni*, or *kay* (pronounced *ké*). Other nouns are preceded by *ang*, *ng* (pronounced *nang*), or *sa*. The use of these particles will be explained in the following section.

Mrs Garcia
  si mrs garcía
John
  si john
the mother
  ang nánay
Mrs Garcia is John's mother.
  si mrs garcía ang nánay ni john

Noun Marking Particles

As explained in the previous section, *ang*, *ng* and *sa* are used to mark nouns which refer to places or things, whereas *si*, *ni* and *kay* mark nouns which refer to proper names or titles.

si & ang

Nouns which are the subject of a sentence are preceded by *si* (names) or *ang* (things). It is important to remember that the subject does not usually appear at the beginning of the sentence. In the following sentences, for example, 'Mrs Garcia' and 'the child' are clearly the subjects, and yet they both appear at the end of their respective sentences.

Mrs Garcia is a teacher.
  títser si mrs garcía
The child is well behaved.
  mabait ang bátà

When a proper name or title is in the first position in the sentence it is preceded by *si*.

My teacher is Mrs Garcia.
  si mrs garcía ang títser ko

If a common noun starts the sentence, it is not generally preceded by anything unless it refers to a specific thing, in which case it is preceded by *ang*.

ng & ni

Words which refer to a possessor are preceded by *ng* or *ni*. The same criterion determine which particle to use as in the case of *si* and *ang*.

Maria's teacher.
   ang títser ni maría
The child's teacher.
   ang títser ng bátà

These same two particles are also used to precede words that refers to the one who performs an action with certain verbs (passive verbs).

Mary saw it.
   nákíta ni maría (literally 'it was seen by Mary')
The child saw it.
   nákíta ng bátà

sa & kay
The particles *sa* or *kay* are used mainly for the meanings 'at, to, on, for' and also after the following prepositions:

because of	*dáhil sa*
for	*pára sa*
concerning	*tungkol sa*
be at	*nása*

Pronouns

I	*ako*
you (singular and familiar)	*ka, ikaw*
he	*siya*
we (including the person being spoken to)	*táyo*
we (excluding the person being spoken to)	*kami*
you (plural, polite)	*kayo*

they	*sila*
this	*ito*
that	*iyan*
that (far away)	*iyon*

The following sentences illustrate the use of some of these pronouns:

I am a teacher.
 títser ako
This is for your mother.
 pára sa nánay mo ito
They are the ones who are going to Manila.
 sila ang púpunta sa maynílà

Special note on *ka*, *ikaw* – 'you'
Ikaw (you) singular is only used as a sentence initiator. For the subject, *ka* is used.

Was it you who came yesterday?
 ikaw ba ang naparíto kahápon?
Did you come yesterday?
 naparíto ka ba kahápon?

Polite form for 'you'
With older people and those you don't know well, the plural form for 'you' should be used, and never the singular. At the same time the politeness particle *hò* (or the even more formal *pò*) should be used.

Are you a teacher, madam?
 títser hó ba kayo?

Did you give it to Pedro, sir?
ibinigay hó ba ninyo kay pédro?

For a child, however, the polite form is never used:

Are you Mrs Garcia's daughter?
anak ka ba ni mrs garcía?

Other pronouns

my	*ko*
your	*mo*
his/her	*niya*
our	*nátin*
our	*námin*
your	*ninyo*
their	*nila*
its	*nito*
its	*niyan*
its	*niyon* or *noon*

to me	*sa ákin*
to you	*sa iyo*
to him/her	*sa kanya*
to us	*sa átin*
to us	*sa ámin*
to you	*sa inyo*
to them	*sa kanila*

Adverbial Expressions

Expressions of time, place, or manner may come at the beginning or at the end of the sentence.

yesterday	*kahápon*
now	*ngayón*
tomorrow	*búkas*
on Monday (past)	*noong lúnes*
on Monday (future)	*sa lúnes*
later	*mámayà*
this evening (later on)	*mámayang gabi*
before	*kanína*
this morning	*kanínang umága*
this noon (past)	*kanínang tangháli*
at three o'clock	*nang alas tres*
here	*díto*
there (not far)	*diyan*
there (far)	*doon*
perhaps	*sigúro*
I hope	*sána*
it might happen	*bakà*

He came yesterday.
  kahápon siya naparíto
He'll go home on Wednesday.
  úuwí siya sa myérkules
I hope you can go there.
  sána makákapunta kayo doon
You might fall.
  baká ka mahúlog

Conjunctions

Common conjunctions are:

and	*at*
but	*péro*
because	*kasi* or *dáhil*
when (future)	*pag* or *kapag*
if	*kung*
when (past)	*noong* or *nang*
even though	*káhit*

Greetings & Civilities

It is easy to strike up a conversation with Filipinos. The people tend to be friendly and not terribly formal, but very respectful of others and considerate of feelings. When speaking with adults one does not know well, or who are of higher status, the speech is inevitably sprinkled with *hò* (as the second word in the sentence) as a sign of respect.

Greetings
Formal
Good morning.
  magandang umága
Good afternoon.
  magandang hápon
Good evening.
  magandang gabi
How are you, sir/madam?
  kumusta hó kayo?
Goodbye.
  paalam

Informal
Hi! or Hello!
  hoy! or *uy!*
Hi Ting, how are you?
  hoy ting, kumusta ka?
Fine! And you?
  mabúti naman! ikaw?

Goodbye.
síge
Goodbye. (when getting off a vehicle)
diyan na kayo (literally 'I'll be leaving you there')
Goodbye. to someone getting off)
diyan ka na or *díto ka na lang*
Let's go.
táyo na

Other Civilities

'Thank you' is not used as much in Pilipino as it is in English. For a service which one expects to be rendered nothing is said (to say 'thank you' would sound sarcastic).

Thank you (very much) sir/madam.
(maráming) salámat
You're welcome.
walang anuman (literally 'it's nothing')

No thanks.
salámat na lang
Don't bother.
hindí bále na lang
Excuse me/sorry. (formal)
ipagpaumanhin ninyo ako
Excuse me/sorry. (colloquial)
ekskyus
Please repeat.
pakiúlit

Note: 'please' is incorporated into the verb with a prefix *paki* – plus the word for 'you' *mo* (familiar) or *hó ninyo* (polite).

Please pass the bread.
  pakipása mo ang tinápay (familiar)
Please pass the bread.
  pakipása hó ninyo ang tinápay (polite)

Forms of Address
Most commonly titles, Mr, Miss, Mrs, Dr, Father, etc, are borrowed directly from English.

My teacher is Mrs Reyes.
  si mrs réyes ang títser ko

Addressing strangers
One uses the title *mámà* for a blue collar man with whom one is not acquainted.

How much are the *atis*?
  magkáno hó ba ang átis, mámà?

A man can say *páre* to a strange man if he wishes to be friendly and intimate.

Excuse me my friend.
  ekskyus lang páre

To a professional man one would say 'sir':

May I ask you a question?
  pwéde hó bang magtanong sir?

For a blue-collar woman a friendly but respectful term of address is *ále* (literally 'auntie'):

How much is a kg of mangoes?
   magkáno hó ba ang kílo ng mangga ále?

For a woman of higher status one uses Miss or Mrs (depending on the age).

Do you have change, Miss?
   may barya hó ba kayo miss?
How much is it in all, madam?
   magkáno ho ba lahat mrs?

Family Terms

This is my	*ito ang .... ko*
father	*tátay*
uncle	*tíyo*
aunt	*tíya*
older brother	*kúya*
older sister	*áte*
friend	*kaibígan*
mother	*nánay*
son/daughter	*anak*
husband/wife	*asáwa*
cousin	*pínsan*
nephew/niece	*pamangkin*

Small Talk

Filipinos are ready to engage in small talk with strangers. It is not unusual to broach subjects which westerners might consider too personal. Try not to act shocked, but do as the Filipinos do. When presented with a question you would rather not answer, remember that in the Philippines there is no strong moral pressure to provide accurate answers.

Many travellers find it convenient from time to time to lie about their age, religion, income or marital status and find safety in talking about offspring that don't exist.

In addressing people of high status or older people the particle *hò* 'sir, madam' should be liberally used and *kayo* 'you' (plural) for 'you' rather than *ka* 'you' (singular).

Are you married?	*may asáwa ka na ba?*
Where are you staying?	*saan ka nakatira?*
I'm staying	*........ lang ako*
in the Manila Hotel	*nása maníla hótel*
on Taft Avenue	*nása taft avenue*

I'm staying with my friend.
  nása báhay ng mga kaibígan ko lang ako

It is all right to ask someone's age:

How old are you?	*ilang taon ka na?*
How old is your son/daughter?	*ilang taon na hó ang anak ninyo?*

I am .... years old.	*ako ay .... ányos/taon*
twenty	*beynte/dalawampung*
twenty-one	*beynte úno/dalawampút isang*
thirty-five	*tréintay síngko/tatlumpút limang*
fifty-four	*singkwéntay kwátro/ limampút ápat na*

Where are you from?	*tagasaan ka?*
Where are you from, sir/madam?	*tagasaan hó kayo?*
I'm from	*taga .... ako*
Germany	*alemánya (dyermani)*
Australia	*awstrálya*
England	*inglatéra*
USA	*isteyts (amérika)*

Other countries are as in English.

I am a	*........ ako*
My father is a	*........ ang tátay ko*
priest	*pári*
police officer	*pulis*
business person	*negosyánte*
teacher	*títser (gúrò)*
student	*istudyánte*
waiter, waitress	*wéyter, wéytres*
nanny	*yáya*

It is all right to ask a person their religion.

What is your religion?	*ano ang relihiyon mo?*
I am	.... *hó ako*
Catholic	*katóliko*
Christian	*kristiyáno*
Protestant	*protestánte*

The Pilipino terms for Hindu, Muslim and Jew are considered to be derogatory. It is, on the other hand, quite acceptable to use the relevant English terms. Most people should understand these.

Feelings

I am	.... *na ako*
tired out	*pagod*
sleepy	*ináantok*
hungry	*gutom*
thirsty	*uhaw*
happy	*masaya*
sad	*malungkot*

Some Useful Phrases

Where is the ....?	*násaan ang ....?*
toilet	*kubéta*
restaurant	*restawran*
cinema	*sinehan*

I am looking for ....
   nagháhanap ako ng ....
I am glad to meet you.
   nagágalak akong makilála ka
Goodbye.
   paálam (formal) or *síge* (informal)

Until we meet again.
  sa súsunod náting pagkikíta
Let's go!
  táyo na!
Can you say that again please?
  pwéde bang pakiúlit?
Can you speak a little more slowly please?
  pwéde bang bagálan mo ang pagsasalitá mo?
Where is the closest telephone?
  saan ba ang may malápit na telépono?
There aren't any.
  walà
They are all gone.
  walá na
There aren't any more mangoes.
  walá nang mangga
There are (still) some.
  méron (pa) or *mayroon (pa)*
There are mangoes.
  may mangga or *me mangga*
Are there any more mangoes?
  may (me) mangga pa ba?
Is there any water?
  may túbig ba?
Is this water drinkable?
  naíinom ba itong túbig?
Wait a minute.
  sandalí lang
I don't know.
  hindí ko alam
I don't understand.
  hindí ko máintindihan

What did you say?
ano ang sinábi mo?
What's the matter?
kumusta ba?
What can I do for you?
ano ang maitútúlong ko sa inyo?
Do you speak Pilipino?
nagsásalitá ka ba ng pilipíno?
I don't know how to speak Pilipino yet.
hindí pa ako marúnong magsalitá ng pilipíno
Excuse me, may I ask you a question?
ekskyus lang hò, pwéde bang magtanong?
Are we in Manila yet?
nása máynilá na ba táyo?
Where are you going?
saan ka púpunta?
Where are we now?
násaan na táyo?

Getting Around

There is an abundance of cheap public transportation available in the Philippines. Jeeps and buses ply almost every passable thoroughfare in the Philippines, and some that are not so passable are nevertheless served. On frequently travelled routes transportation is always available, but in remote areas it is better to enquire. The fares are set, but if you are doubtful, it would be wise to ask a fellow passenger.

If you are going to a destination slightly off the route, the driver might take you there for a small additional fee. On buses there are normally conductors who provide tickets. On jeeps the fare is given directly to the driver. On the long distance routes from Manila air-conditioned coaches are available. Long-distance buses have a schedule, but most buses and jeeps do not follow a schedule and leave when they have a load. They can be hailed anywhere, and as long as they are not full, they will stop. They also let passengers off almost anywhere along the route.

Is this taxi free (available)?
pwéde bang masakyan ang táksing ito?
Take me to this address.
dalhin ninyo ako so lugar na ito
Do you go to Quezon city?
pumúpunta ba kayo sa quézon city?
Stop!
pára hò!

Stop ....!   *pára na hó ....!*
  here   *díto*
  at the corner   *sa kánto*

Tell me when we get to Luneta Park.
  pakisábi mo sa ákin kung dumating na táyo sa lunéta park
How much is the fare?
  magkáno hó ang pamasáhe?
How much is it to Taft Avenue?
  magkáno hó hanggang sa taft avenue?
Here's the fare.
  báyad hò
Wasn't it two pesos to Taft Avenue?
  hindí ba dalawang píso hanggang taft avenue?
Does this bus leave soon?
  malapit na bang umalis itong bus?
Where do I get the bus for Los Baños?
  saan hó ang sákáyan papuntang los báños?
I want to get off at Luneta Park.
  gusto kong bumabá sa lunéta park
Are we at Makati yet?
  nása makáti na ba táyo?
What time will the bus leave?
  ánong óras áalis itong bus?
Does the bus for Baguio leave from this station?
  díto ba nanggágáling ang mga bus na papuntang báguio?
Which station does the bus for Baguio leave from?
  saang istasyon umáalis ang mga bus na papuntang báguio?
Is there an air-conditioned bus that goes to Los Baños?
  may bus bang air-con na papuntang los báños?

Can I buy a ticket on the ....?	*pwéde ba sa .... na lang ako bumili ng tíket?*
bus	*bus*
train	*tren*
boat	*barko*

Where can I buy a .... in advance? (literally 'reserve a ....')	*saan ako pwéding magresérba ng ....?*
ticket	*tíket*
a seat	*úpúan*
a cabin	*kamaróte*

What time does the boat arrive?
  anong óras dárating ang barko?
Will the train arrive after dark?
  madilim na ba pagdating ng tren?
Will it still be dark when the boat arrives?
  madilim pa ba pagdating ng bárko?
Is it unsafe to get off the boat while it is still dark?
  delikádo bang bumabá ng barko hanggang madilim pa?
Is there a place for tourists to stay in Lucena City?
  may matútulúyan ba ang mga turísta sa lucéna city?
Is there a place that is cheaper than a 1st-class hotel?
  may mas múra pa ba sa first-class hotel?
Is there a place to buy souvenirs?
  may mabíbilhan ba ng súbenirs?

What do I take to get ....?	*ano ang pwéde kong sakyan ....?*
from the pier to town	*papuntang plása mulá sa piyer*
to Ormoc City	*papuntang ormoc city*

Some Useful Phrases

Is it dangerous to swim here?
hindí ba delikádong lumangoy díto?
Where can I change my money?
saan ako pwédeng magpapalit ng péra?
When is the (last) bus to Bontoc?
anong óras áalis ang (huling) bus papuntang bontoc?
Are there any buses after 4 pm?
paglípas nang alas kwátro (ng hápon) walá na bang bus?
Is there a bus at 5 am?
nang alas síngko (nang umága) may bus na ba?
Does the bus to Bontoc go through Sagada?
dumáraan ba sa sagáda ang bus papuntang bontoc?

Where is the ....?	*nasaan ang ....?*
bus station	*terminal ng bus*
train station	*terminal ng tren*
bus station for the Baguio buses	*terminal ng mga bus na papuntang báguio*
post office	*post ópis*
the road to Bontoc	*daan papuntang bontoc*

Is the bus station far?
maláyó ba ang terminal ng bus?

The road to Banawe is	*ang daan papunta sa*
	banawe ay ....
straight ahead	*dirétso lámang*
to the right	*papakánan*
to the left	*papakaliwà*

Go straight to the store and then turn right.
  dumirétso ka hanggang sa tindáhan at pagkatápos ay lumikó ka sa kánan
The bank is behind the city hall.
  ang bángko ay násaad likod ng city hall
The bank is facing the city hall.
  ang bángko ay kaharap ng city hall
Go back to the gas station.
  bumalik ka sa gásolinahan
The road to Umali Subdivision is 50 metres further.
  ang kálye papuntang umáli subdivision ay limampung métro pa kaláyò
Do you go all the way to Cainta or must I transfer?
  púpunta ba kayo hanggang caintá o kailángan ko hó bang lumípat?
Where do I get off to catch the bus to Cainta?
  saan ako bábabá pára makakúha ng bus papuntang caintà?
Where does the jeep for Cainta stop?
  saan ba tumítigil ang dyip papuntang caintà?

Accommodation

Finding Accommodation

Where can one ....?	*saan hó ba díto pwédeng ....?*
find a hotel	*makákíta ng hotel*
spend the night	*magpalípas ng gabi*
Where is the .... hotel here?	*saan hó ba díto ang .... hotel?*
best	*pinakamagandang*
cheapest	*pinakamúrang*

Is that the cheapest place (hotel) to spend the night?
iyon na hó ba ang pinakamúrang lugar (hotel) na pwéde kong tulúgan?

Is it (that hotel) clean?
malínis hó ba doon (iyong hotel na iyon)?

Where is the bathroom?
násaan hó ba díto ang kubéta (toilet)?

Does the room have a private bath?
*may saríling **c r** ba iyong kwárto?*

Do you have rooms with a private bath?
mayroon hó ba kayong kwárto na may saríling toilet (kubéta)?

At the Hotel

Can I please see the room?
pwéde ko hó bang mákíta ang kwárto?
Please turn the air-conditioner (fan) on.
pakibuksan hó ang air-con (béntilador)
Please turn the lights off.
pakipatay hó ang ílaw

I need a (another)	*pwéde hó bang makahingí ng (isa pang) ....*
towel	*twálya*
bar of soap	*sabon*
face cloth	*bímpo*
bottle of water	*bóte ng túbig*
lamp	*lámsyed*
mosquito coil	*katol*

My room is too dark.
madilim hó yátá itong áking kwárto
Can you drink the water (from the tap)?
pwéde hó bang inumin iyong túbig (sa grípo)?

Put some drinking water	*pakidala ngá hó ng túbig na ínúmin ....*
in my room	*díto sa kwárto*
on the table	*díto sa lamésa*

These .... are not clean.	*madumi hó yátá itong mga ....*
pillow cases	*punda*
sheets	*kúmot*

Please change them.
pwéde hó bang pakipalitan
Isn't it extra for two in the room?
mé ékstrang báyad hó ba kung dalawa kami díto sa kwárto?
Do you have a room with two beds?
méron hó ba kayong kwártong mé dalawang káma?
Do you have a room with a double bed?
méron hó ba kayong kwártong mé kámang pangdalawáhan?

How much is it for ....?	*magkáno hó ba ang báyad pára sa ....?*
one night	*isang gabi*
a week	*linggo*
two people	*dalawang táo*

Are .... included in that price?	*kasáma na hó ba ang .... sa báyad?*
meals	*pagkáin*
breakfast	*agáhan*
lunch	*tanghalían*
dinner	*hapúnan*
afternoon tea	*meriénda*

Please do not disturb me.
hwag hó (sána) akong istórbohin
Please make up the room now.
pwéde hó bang pakilínis múna ang kwárto ngayon?
Can you serve me breakfast in my room?
pwéde hó bang magpadala ng agáhan díto sa áking kwárto?

Please wake me up at	*pakigísing ngá hó ako nang ....*
6 am	*alas sais nang umága*
7.30	*alas syéte i médya*
5.45	*alas síngko kwaréntay síngko*

How do I get from here to the ....?	*paáno hó ba ako makákarating sa ....?*
airport	*airport*
train station	*istasyon ng tren*
bus terminal	*terminal ng bus*

Do you have a map of the town?
méron hó ba kayong mápa nitong báyan?
Are there any taxis?
méron hó ba dítong mga táksi?

Payment
Can you change my travellers' cheque?
nagpápalit hó ba kayo ng travellers cheque?
Please let me have the bill.
magkáno hó ang bábayáran ko
There is a mistake in the bill.
méron hó yátang malí díto sa bill
I did not eat my breakfast here yesterday.
hindí hó ako díto kumáin ng agáhan kahápon

Can I pay with ....?	*tumátanggap hó ba kayo ....?*
a travellers' cheque	*ng travellers cheque*
credit cards	*ng credit cards*

Some Useful Words

bed
  káma
clean
  malínis
cold
  malamig
dirty
  marumi
drinking glass
  báso
hot
  maínit
key
  súsi
lock
  kandádo
noisy
  maíngay
quiet
  tahímik
restaurant
  karindérya
wardrobe
  aparador
water
  túbig
window
  bintánà

Food

In a Restaurant

Can we get .... here now?
    pwéde ba táyong ....
    díto ngayon?

food	*kumáin*
lunch	*magtanghalían*
breakfast	*mag-agáhan*
supper	*maghapúnan*

Is it self-service?
    ako ba ang kúkúha?
What kind of dishes do you have?
    anu-ano ang mga pagkáin ninyo díto?

Reading a menu

The following are typical dishes in many parts of the Philipines. Some of them are sure to appear on the menu in any local eating house.

adobong pusit	squid with coconut milk in its own ink
aso	dog – a local favourite
balut (penoy)	a 'hard boiled' duck egg with embryo
ginatan	sweet stew of root crops and bananas in coconut milk
kilawan pusit	raw squid marinated in coconut milk, garlic, salt and peppercorns

lechon	suckling pig in a liver based sauce – often eaten at festivals
lumpia shanghai	spring rolls
tahong	green mussels cooked in sauce
talaba	raw oysters marinated in vinegar and garlic

Let me have	*bigyan mo ako ng ....*
Could I have some .... ?	*pwéde ba n'yo akong bigyan ng .... ?*
Do you have ....?	*méron ba kayong ....?*
I would like some	*gusto ko ng ....*

Seafood

bouillabaisse	*sinigang*
clams	*tulya*
crabs	*alimásag*
fish (fried)	*(prítong) isdà*
lobster	*ulang*
milkfish	*bangus*
mussels	*tahong*
oysters	*talaba*
shrimp	*hípon*

Meat, Eggs & Dairy Products

beef (grilled)	*(iníhaw na) karneng báka*
chicken	*manók*
pork	*(karneng) báboy*
eggs (fried)	*prítong itlog*
soft-boiled eggs	*malasádong itlog*

hard-boiled eggs	*nilágang itlog*
scrambled eggs	*tórtang itlog*
butter	*mantikílya*
cheese	*késo*
milk	*gátas*

Fruit & Vegetables

Fruits	*prútas*
avocado	*abokádo*
banana	*ságing*
custard apple	*átis*
durian	*durian*
jackfruit	*langka*
kalamansi	*calamondin kalamansi*
lanson	*lanzónes*
mango	*mangga*
mangosteen	*mangostan*
papaya	*papáya*
pineapple	*pinya*
pomelo	*suhà*
rambutan	*rambutan*
tomato	*kamátis*
watermelon	*pakwan*

Vegetables	*gúlay*
bamboo shoots	*labóng*
cabbage	*repólyo*
chilli pepper	*síli*
chinese cabbage	*pétsay*
egg plant	*talóng*
garlic	*báwang*
mushroom	*kabuti*

onion	*sibúyas*
palm heart	*úbod*
squash	*kalabása*
radish	*labanós*
taro	*gábi*

Bread

bread	*tinápay*
rolls	*pandesal*
sandwiches	*sanwits*
toast	*tustádo*

Drinks

coffee	*kape*
tea	*tsaa*
avocado drink	*abokádo dyus*
mango drink	*mangga dyus*
lemonade	*lemonáda*
ice water	*túbig na may yélo*
beer	*beer*

Snacks, Sauces & Soups

broth	*sabaw*
fish sauce	*patis*
noodles	*bíhon*
peanuts	*maní*
porridge	*lúgaw*
shrimp paste	*bagoong*
soup	*sópas*
fish soup	*sinigang na isdà*
pork soup	*sinigang na báboy*
soy sauce	*tóyò*

Vegetarian Food

Filipino cooking uses meat, animal fat, fish sauce or shrimp paste as a condiment for vegetables, therefore it is often very difficult to find strictly vegetarian food. A simple statement that one does not eat meat or fish or shrimp, etc, is not necessarily going to get the desired results. The best suggestion for people who definitely want to stick to a vegetarian diet is to claim to be allergic to anything even vaguely meat based. This is sure to increase your chances of actually getting hold of proper vegetarian food.

I am allergic to ....
    alérdyik ako sa ....
Does this have .... in it?
    méron ba itong ....?
I cannot eat meat.
    hindí makakáin ng kárne
I don't eat meat.
    hindí ako kumákáin ng kárne
I am a vegetarian.
    mga gúlay lang ang kinákáin ko
    (literally 'Vegetables are the only thing I eat.')
I can only eat vegetables and fish.
    mga gúlay at isdá lang ang nakákáin ko
I can't eat dairy products.
    hindí ako makakáin ng mga pagkáing yárí mulá sa gátas
    (literally 'foods made from milk')
I can eat rice.
    nakákakáin ako ng kánin

Some Useful Phrases

I'll just have something easy to digest.
  yung madaling matúnaw na lang ang ákin

What kind of noodles do you have?
  anong kláseng bíhon ang méron?

What is *mámi?*
  ano ba yung mámi?

Is *mámi* the same as *pansit?*
  parého ba ang mámi sa pansit?

Is there a broth with the bean threads?
  méron bang sabaw ang sotanghon?

Do you have anything other than sausage?
  méron ba kayong iba búkod sa soríso?

Is this fish fresh or from a can?
  ito bang isdang ito ay saríwá o deláta?

Shopping

Filipinos normally bargain. It is not considered bad form to ask for a lower price, and small-scale vendors never really expect to get the first price offered – even for small purchases. In big stores the prices are normally fixed.

Where can I buy ....?	*saan ako makákabili ....?*
a bus ticket	*ng tíket ng bus*
a newspaper	*ng diyaryo*
a razor	*ng pang-áhit*
soap	*ng sabon*
toilet paper	*ng tísyu*

How much are the ....?	*magkáno hó ang mga ....?*
mangoes	*mangga*
bananas	*ságing*
apples	*mansánas*
umbrellas	*páyong*

Eight pesos a piece.
  walong píso isa
Too expensive!
  masyádong mahal!
Make it 10 for two.
  sampung píso na lang itong dalawa
What are these?
  ano ang mga ito?
How much is this?
  magkána hó ito?

Are the mangoes ....?	.... ang mga mangga?
ripe	*hinog na ba*
sweet	*matatamis ba*
unripe	*hilaw pa ba*

Some Useful Phrases

Where is the market?
násaan ang paléngke?

Do you have any ....?
méron hó ba kayong ....?

Could you show me another one?
pwéde ba ninyo akong pakitáin ng iba?

Could you show me another room?
pwéde ba ninyo akong pakitáin ng ibang kwárto?

This is too big/small.
masyádong malaki/maliit ito

I want a less expensive one.
gusto ko ng mas múra

Please wrap the shirt.
pakibálot ang kamiséta

Isn't it possible to get a reduction?
walá na bang táwad? or *hindí ba pwedeng tumáwad?*

No it's not.
walá na (hindí na pwéde)

How much is it for a dozen?
magkáno hó ba ang isang doséna?

How many are you taking?
ilan ba ang kúkúnin nyo?

Only one (of course).
(syémpre) isa lang

Do you have a plastic bag (to put this in)?
may plástik ba kayo (pára paglagyan nito)?

Some Useful Words

batteries
  batería
book
  libro
cigarettes
  sigarílyo
comb
  suklay
dictionary
  diksionáryo
earrings
  híkaw
envelopes
  sóbre
fan
  paypay
flashlight
  lénte
map of the Philippines
  mápa ng pilipínas
matches
  pósporo
mirror
  salamin

needle
  karáyom
paper
  papel
pen (ballpoint)
  bolpoin
ring
  singsing
thread
  sinúlid
toothbrush
  sipílyo or *tútbras*
toothpaste
  kólgeit

Colours
black
  itim
blue
  asul
brown
  kape
green
  bérde
red
  pula
tan
  kayumanggi
white
  puti
yellow
  dilaw

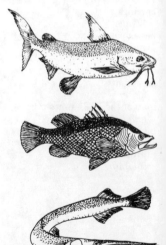

Size, Length & Weight

big, large
  malaki
small
  maliit
medium, in between
  katamtáman
larger
  mas malaki
smaller
  mas maliit
heavy
  mabigat
light
  magaan
long
  mahábà
short
  maiklì

Health

Medical service is widely available, especially in larger towns. It is almost entirely private, and prices for service can range from the reasonable to the shockingly expensive. The quality of medical service varies greatly. Some of the doctors have had specialised training and advanced residency abroad. Others practice after minimum training in provincial schools of not very high standards. In short, one has to be careful with doctors, but very good medical service is available.

Complaints

I seem to have	*párang .... ako*
I have	*........ ako*
anaemia	*may anémya* or
	kakulangan sa dugó
asthma	*may híkà*
athlete's foot	*may alipunga*
a broken arm	*may bálí sa braso*
a broken leg	*may bálí sa páa*
a cold	*may sipon*
cough	*may ubo*
cramps	*may pulíkat*
diabetes	*may diyabétis*
diarrhoea	*nagtátae*
a fever	*may lagnat*
an infection	*may impeksyon*
pneumonia	*may pulmunya*
prickly heat	*may búngang áraw*

sunburn	*may súnog ng áraw (sa balat)*
a wound	*may súgat*

At the Chemist

Do you have ....?	*méron ba kayong ....?*
adhesive tape	*pláster*
antibiotics	*antibayótiks*
antiseptic	*antiséptik*
aspirin	*aspirin*
bandaids	*korítas*
condoms	*kondom*
contraceptives	*pangkóntra sa pagdadalang-táo*
cotton balls	*búlak*
gauze	*gása*
medicine for a tooth ache	*gamot sa masakit na ngípin*
pain killer	*pang-alis ng sakit*
rubbing alcohol	*alkohol na panghaplos*
sleeping tablets	*pampatúlog na tablétas*
tampons	*tampon*

Do I need a prescription to buy antibiotic ointment?
kailángan ko ba ng reséta pára makabili ng pamáhid na antibayótik?

Do you have something for diarrhoea?
may pangkóntra hó ba kayo sa pagtatae?

Do you have medicine for asthma?
may gamot hó ba kayo sa híkà?

Do you have mosquito repellant?
may pampáhid hó ba kayo lában sa lamok?

At the Doctor

Where can I see a doctor?
  saan ako pwédeng magpagamot?
I have been vomiting.
  nagsúsuka ako
I am in pain.
  may masakit sa ákin
I am pregnant.
  nagdádalang-táo ako
I have dysentry.
  nagtátae ako

I've got pain in the	masakit ang áking ....
arms	*bráso*
back	*likod*
chest	*dibdib*
ears	*ténga*
eyes	*mga mata*
feet, legs	*mga páa*
hands	*mga kamay*
head	*úlo*
nose	*ilong*
stomach	*tiyan*
teeth	*ngípin*
throat	*lalamúnan*

Some Useful Phrases

Where is the doctor?
  násaan ang doktor?
Where is the dentist?
  saan ba may dentísta?
Where is the hospital?
  násaan ang uspital?
Please call a doctor.
  pakitáwag ng doktor
I am allergic to penicillin.
  alérdyik ako sa penísilin
I cannot sleep.
  hindí ako mákatulog
Is it serious?
  malubhá ba iyon?

Numbers

Counting

There are two sets of numbers: the native Pilipino and the Spanish. The Spanish numbers are used for time, dates, and with prices above 10. Pilipino numbers are used for quantities. English numbers are also widely used.

	Spanish	Pilipino
1	*úno*	*isa*
2	*dos*	*dalawa*
3	*tres*	*tatlo*
4	*kwátro*	*ápat*
5	*síngko*	*lima*
6	*sais, seis*	*ánim*
7	*syéte*	*pito*
8	*ótso*	*walo*
9	*nwébe*	*siyam*
10	*diyes*	*sampù*
11	*ónse*	*labing isa*
12	*dóse*	*labing dal'wa*
13	*trése*	*labing tatlo*
14	*katórse*	*labing apat*
15	*kínse*	*labing lima*
16	*diyesiseis*	*labing anim*
17	*diyesisyéte*	*labing pito*
18	*diyesiótso*	*labing walo*
19	*diyesinwébe*	*labing siyam*
20	*béynte, bénte*	*dalawampù*

21	*béynteúno*	*dalawampút isa*
30	*tréynta, trénta*	*tatlumpù*
40	*kwarénta*	*apatnapù*
50	*singkwénta*	*limampù*
60	*sisénta*	*ánimnapù*
70	*siténta*	*pitumpù*
80	*otsénta*	*walumpù*
90	*nobénta, nubénta*	*siyamnapù*
100	*syénto*	*isandaan*
1000	*mil*	*libo*
1,000,000	*milyon*	*ángaw*

Money & Quantities

Prices containing only the number 10 or under are usually given with Pilipino. Prices containing higher numbers are given with Spanish numbers. The word *peso* is *píso* with Pilipino numbers and *pésos* with Spanish numbers.

three pesos	*tatlong píso*
fifteen pesos	*kínse pésos*

Pilipino numbers are used for quantities, but above 10 Spanish numbers are used too.

How much do .... cost?	*magkáno ang ....?*
15	*labing lima/kínse*
100	*isandaan/syénto*
a dozen	*isang doséna*

This costs	*ito ay ....*
two pesos	*dalawang píso/dos pésos*
25 pesos	*beyntesíngko pésos*

Time & Dates

Time

What time is it?
anong óras na?
It is one o'clock.
ala úna na
It is ten o'clock.
alas diyes na
half past one
ala úna'y médya
one fifteen
ala úna kínse
a quarter to five
ménos kínse pára alas síngko

Days

These words are of Spanish origin except for the word for Sunday.

Monday
  lúnes
Tuesday
  mártes
Wednesday
  myérkules
Thursday
  hwébes
Friday
  byérnes
Saturday
  sábado
Sunday
  linggo

Some useful phrases

I came here on Sunday.
  nagpunta ako díto noong linggo
I will leave on Tuesday.
  áalis ako sa mártes
I will only spend two days here.
  dal'wang araw lang ako díto

I will spend .... in Baguio	.... *ako sa báguio*
a week	*isang linggo*
a month	*isang buwan*
three months	*tatlong buwan*
a year	*isang taon*

Months

January
enéro
February
pebréro
March
márso
April
abril
May
máyo
June
húnyo
July
húlyo
August
agósto
September
setyémbre
October
oktúbre
November
nobyémbre
December
disyémbre

Vocabulary

A

accept – *tanggap*
  Do you accept cheques? – *tumátanggap ba kayo ng tséke?*
ache – *sakit*
adhesive tape – *pláster*
afraid – *takot*
afternoon – *hápon*
  good afternoon – *magandang hápon*
afternoon tea – *meriénda*
again – *úlit*
alcohol – *alkohol*
alcoholic drinks – *álak*
all – *lahat*
all gone – *walá na*
allergic – *alérdyik*
already – *na*
also – *din, rin*
and – *at*
another one – *isa pa*
antibiotic – *antibayótik*
antiseptic – *antiséptiko*
apple – *mansánas*
April – *abril*
arm – *bráso*
ask (a question) – *tanong*
ask for – *hingì*
athlete's foot – *alipunga*

August – *agósto*
aunt – *tíya*
Australia – *awstrálya*
awake – *gising na*

B
back – *likod*
bag – *bag*
   plastic bag – *plástik*
banana – *ságing*
bandaids – *korítas*
bank – *bángko*
batteries – *bateríya*
be (at a place) – *nása*
beautiful – *maganda*
because – *kasi, dáhil*
bed – *káma*
beer – *beer*
before – *kanína*
besides – *bukod sa*
best – *pinakamabúti*
better – *mas mabúti*
big – *malaki*
black – *maitim*
blanket – *kúmot*
blue – *asul*
boat – *bapor, barko*
book – *libro*
bottle – *bóte*
   bottle of water – *bóte ng túbig*
bouillabaisse – *sinigang*
bread – *tinápay*

break – *báli*
breakfast – *agáhan*
  eat breakfast – *mag-agáhan*
bring – *dala*
  please bring – *pakidala*
  have someone bring – *magpadala*
broil/grill – *íhaw*
  broiled – *iníhaw*
broth – *sabaw*
bus – *bus*
but – *péro*
buy – *bili*
  can buy – *makabili*
  place to buy – *mabíbilhan*
by now – *na*

C
cabin – *kamaróte, kábin*
canned – *de láta*
car – *kótse*
catholic – *katóliko*
change (small money) – *bárya*
change (v) – *palitan*
  please change – *pakipalitan*
cheap – *múra*
  cheapest – *pinakamúra*
chest – *dibdib*
child – *bátà*
Christian – *kristiyáno*
cigarettes – *sigarílyo*
city hall – *city hall*
clams – *tulya*

clean – *línis, malínis*
  please make up (the room) – *pakilínis (ang kwárto)*
cloth – *téla*
cold – *sipon*
  have a cold – *sinísipon*
comb – *suklay*
come – *dating, paríto*
  is coming – *dumárating*
  will come – *dárating*
  came – *dumating, naparíto*
come from – *gáling*
corner – *kánto*
cotton balls – *búlak*
cousin – *pínsan*
crabs – *alimásag*

D

dangerous – *delikádo*
dark – *dilim, madilim*
date – *pétsa*
daughter, son – *anak*
December – *disyémbre*
delicious – *masarap*
diarrhoea (to have) – *nagtátae*
dictionary – *diksionáryo*
dinner – *hapúnan*
  eat dinner – *maghapúnan*
dirt – *dumi*
  dirty – *madumi*
distance – *láyò, kalayúan*
  distant – *maláyò*

disturb – *istórbohin*
  disturbance – *istórbo*
doctor – *doktor*
  see a doctor – *magpagamot*
do not – *huwag*
double – *pandalawáhan*
  double bed – *kámang pandalawáhan*
  double room – *kwártong pandalawáhan*
dozen – *doséna*
drink – *inom*
drowsiness, sleepiness – *antok*
  drowsy – *ináantok na*

E

ear – *ténga*
earrings – *híkaw*
eat – *káin*
  ate – *kumáin*
eatery – *karindérya*
England – *inglatéra, inggland*
envelope – *sóbre*
even though – *káhit*
evening – *gabi*
  good evening – *magandang gabi*
  this evening (later on) – *mámayang gabi*
excuse me, sorry – *paumanhin, ekskyus*
  excuse me, sorry (formal) – *ipagpaumanhin ninyo ako*
  excuse me, sorry (informal) – *ekskyus (ho)*
expensive – *mahal*
  It's too expensive – *masyádong mahal*
  extra – *ékstra*

F

face cloth – *bímpo*
faeces – *táe*
fall – *mahúlog*
fan – *paypay*
far – *maláyò*
fare – *pamasáhe, pasáhe*
father – *tátay*
fatigue – *pagkapágod*
  fatigued – *pagod*
faucet – *grípo*
February – *pebréro*
fever – *lagnat*
  have a fever – *nilálagnat, may lagnat*
fine – *mabúti*
first – *múna, úna*
fish – *ísdà*
fish sauce – *patis*
five – *lima, síngko*
flashlight – *lénte*
food – *pagkáin*
for – *pára*
forty – *apatnapù, kwarénta*
four – *ápat, kwátro*
fourteen – *labing ápat, katórse*
fracture – *balì*
fresh – *saríwà*
Friday – *byérnes*
friend – *kaibígan*
from – *mulà*
fruits – *prútas*

G

gasoline – *gasolína*
gas station – *gasolinahan*
gauze – *gása*
Germany – *alemánya, dyérmani*
get – *kúha*
  will get – *kúkúha*
  get it – *kúnin*
  get off (a vehicle) – *bábà*
  get on (a vehicle) – *sakay*
give – *bigay*
  give me – *bigyan*
  give it – *ibigay*
  gave it – *ibinigay*
go – *punta*
gold – *gintò*
good – *mabúti*
  good afternoon – *magandang hápon*
  good evening – *magandang gabi*
  good morning – *magandang umága*
goodbye – *paálam* (formal), *síge* (informal)
green – *bérde*
grill/broil – *íhaw*

H

happy – *masaya, tuwà*
have – *mayroon, may*
  have a cold – *sinísipon, may sipon*
  have diarrhoea – *nagtátae*
  have a fever – *nilálagnat, may lagnat*
  don't have – *walà*
head – *úlo*

here – *díto*
help – *túlong*
  Can you help me? – *pwéde ba akong pakitulúngan?*
hi/hello – *hoy, uy*
hope – *pag-ása*
hour – *óras*
house – *báhay*
how – *paáno*
  How much? – *magkáno*
  How are (you)? – *kumusta?*
  How is your mother? – *kumusta ang nánay mo?*
  How many? – *ilan?*
  How old are you? – *ilang taon ka na?*
hungry – *gutom na*
  have hunger – *nagúgutom*
husband, wife – *asáwa*

I

ice – *yélo*
if – *kung*
include – *isáma*
  breakfast included – *kasáma ang agáhan*
infection – *impeksiyon*

J

January – *enéro*
jeep – *dyip*
job – *trabáho*
July – *húlyo*
June – *húnyo*

K

kilogram – *kílo*
kind – *kláse*
know – *alam*
  I don't know. – *hindí ko alam*
  know how to – *marúnong*
knowledge – *alam*
knowledge (ability) – *dúnong*

L

lamp – *lámsyed*
language – *wíkà*
last – *huli*
  last bus – *huling bus*
later – *mámayà*
leave – *alis*
  will leave – *áalis*
leg – *binti*
left (side) – *kaliwà*
left (over) – *nátira*
like – *gusto*
like (similar) – *parého*
liquor – *álak*
lobster – *ulang*
look at – *tingnan*
look for – *hanápin*
lunch – *tanghalían*
  to eat lunch – *magtanghalían*

M

man – *táo*
  (blue collar) man – *mámà*

map – *mápa*
March – *márso*
married – *may asáwa*
  Are you married? – *may asáwa ka na ba?*
matches – *pósporo*
may (can) – *pwéde*
May – *máyo*
medicine – *gamot*
metre – *métro*
might – *bakà*
milkfish – *bangus*
minute – *minúto*
  wait a minute – *sandalí lang*
mirror – *salamin*
mistake – *malì, sálà*
Monday – *lúnes*
money – *péra*
month – *buwan*
morning – *umága*
  good morning – *magandang umága*
  this morning – *kanínang umága*
mother – *nánay*
move it – *ilípat*
moviehouse – *sinehan*
munchies – *pulútan*
mussels – *tahong*

N

name – *pangálan*
  What is your name? (to adult) – *ano hó ang pangálan nyo?*
  What is you name? (to child) – *ano ang pangálan mo?*

nanny – *yáya*
near – *malápit*
  near the moviehouse – *sa may sinehan*
need – *kailángan*
needle – *karáyom* nephew, niece – *pamangkin*
newspaper – *dyáryo*
never – *hindì*
niece, nephew – *pamangkin*
noodles – *bíhon, míswa*
noon – *tangháli*
nothing – *walà*
November – *nobyémbre*
now – *ngayon*
  by now – *na*

O

occupation – *trabáho*
October – *oktúbre*
of course – *syémpre*
ointment – *pamáhid*
old (person) – *matandà*
old (thing) – *lúmà*
older brother – *kúya*
older sister – *áte*
one more – *isa pa*
only – *lang*
other than – *bukod sa*
oysters – *talaba*

P

pain – *sakit*
paper – *papel*

pass – *pása*
  Please pass the bread. – *pakipása ang tinápay*
payment – *báyad*
pay – *magbáyad*
  amount to be paid – *bábayáran*
  Here's the payment. – *báyad hò*
peanuts – *mani*
pen (ballpoint) – *bolpoin*
perhaps – *sigúro*
peso – *píso*
petrol – *gasolína*
pier – *piyer*
pillow – *únan*
pillow case – *punda*
place – *lugar*
plastic bag – *plástik*
porridge – *lúgaw*
post office – *pos ópis*
policeman – *pulis*
prescription – *reséta*
prickly heat – *búngang áraw*
priest – *pári*
private – *saríli*
  private bath – *saríling **c r**, toilet*
Protestant – *protestánte*

Q

question – *tanong*
  ask a question – *magtanong*

R

razor – *pang-áhit*
red – *pula, mapula*
religion – *relihiyon*
repeat – *úlit*
reserve – *resérba*
restaurant – *karindérya*
ride – *sakay*
right – *kánan*
right (correct) – *támà*
ring – *singsing*
ripe – *hinog*
road – *daan*
room – *kwárto*
rubbing alcohol – *alkohol na panghaplos*

S

sad – *malungkot*
same – *parého*
sandwich – *sánwits*
Saturday – *sábado*
sausage – *soríso*
say – *sábi*
  was said – *sinábi*
seat – *úpúan*
see – *makákíta*
  saw it – *nákíta*
September – *setyémbre*
service station – *gásolinahan*
sheet – *kúmot*
shirt – *kamiséta*
shoes – *sapátos*

shrimp – *hípon*
shrimp paste – *bagoong*
silver – *pílak*
sit – *upò*
sleep – *túlog*
  is sleeping – *natútúlog*
  fell asleep – *nákatúlog*
  will sleep – *matútúlog*
  put to sleep – *pinatúlog*
  sleeping on – *tinútulúgan*
  (be) sleepy – *ináantok*
  sleepiness – *antok*
soap – *sabon*
son – *anak*
soon – *malápit na*
soup – *sópas, sabaw*
  fish soup – *sinigang*
souvenir – *subenir*
soy sauce – *tóyò*
speak – *magsalità*
spend the night – *magpalípas ng gabi, tulúgan*
sprain – *pilay*
station – *istasyon, terminal*
  train station – *istasyon ng tren*
  bus station – *terminal ng bus*
  petrol station – *gásolinahan*
stay – *tira*
  staying – *nakatira*
stomach – *tiyan*
stop – *tígil*
store – *tindáhan*

straight – *dirétso*
  straight ahead – *dirétso lámang*
student – *istudyánte*
Sunday – *linggo*
sweet – *matamis*
swim – *langoy*

T

table – *lamésa, mésa*
tap – *grípo*
tap water – *túbig sa grípo*
taxi – *táksi*
teacher – *títser*
telephone – *telépono*
terminal – *terminal, istasyon*
thanks – *salámat*
  thank you – *salámat hó sa inyo*
  no thanks – *salámat na lang*
there (far) – *doon*
there (not far) – *diyan*
  there is, are – *may, mayroon*
  there are (still) some – *mayroon (pa)/méron (pa)*
  there aren't any more – *walá na*
thirst – *úhaw*
  thirsty – *uhaw na*
this – *ito*
these – *ang mga ito*
thousand – *líbo, mil*
thread – *sinúlid*
throat – *lalamúnan*
Thursday – *hwébes*
ticket – *tíket*

time – *óras*
  What time is it? – *anong óras na ngayon?*
tired (out) – *pagod*
tired (sleepy) – *ináantok*
to – *sa*
toilet – *kubéta*
toilet paper – *tisyu*
tomorrow – *búkas*
tooth – *ngípin*
  tooth ache – *masakit na ngípin*
toothbrush – *sipílyo* or *tútbras*
toothbrush – *kólgeit*
tourist – *turísta*
towel – *twálya*
town – *báyan*
train – *tren*
transfer – *lípat*
Tuesday – *mártes*
turn – *lumikò*
  turn left – *lumikó sa kaliwà*

U
umbrella – *páyong*
understand – *intindi*
  can understand – *máintindihan*
United States – *isteyts, amérika, estádos unídos*
unripe – *hilaw*
unsafe – *delikádo*

V
very – *masyádo*

W

wait – *hintay, maghintay*
  Wait a minute. – *sandalí lang*
waiter, waitress – *wéyter, wéytres*
wake up – *gísing*
  Please wake me up. – *pakigísing ako*
wash cloth – *bímpo*
water – *túbig*
Wednesday – *myérkules*
week – *linggo*
what – *ano*
when – *kailan, kélan*
where – *saan*
  Where are we now? – *nasaan na táyo*
  Where are you from? – *taga saan ka?*
while – *samantálà*
  a while ago – *kanína*
white – *putì*
who – *síno*
why – *bákit*
wife – *asáwa*
woman – *babáe*
word – *salità*
wound – *súgat*
wrap – *bálot*

Y

year – *taon, ányo*
yellow – *dilaw*
yesterday – *kahápon*
yet – *pa*
  not yet – *hindí pa*

Language Survival Kits

Complete your travel experience with a Lonely Planet phrasebook. Developed for the independent traveller, the phrasebooks enable you to communicate confidently in any practical situation – and get to know the local people and their culture.

Skipping lengthy details on where to get your drycleaning ironed, information in the phrasebooks covers bargaining, customs and protocol, how to address people and introduce yourself, explanations of local ways of telling the time, dealing with bureaucracy and bargaining, plus plenty of ways to share your interests and learn from locals.

Australian
Introduction to Australian English, Aboriginal and Torres Strait languages.
Arabic (Egyptian)
Arabic (Moroccan)
Brazilian
Burmese
Cantonese
Central Europe
Covers Czech, French, German, Hungarian, Italian and Slovak.
Eastern Europe
Covers Bulgarian, Czech, Hungarian, Polish, Romanian and Slovak.
Fijian
Hindi/Urdu
Indonesian
Japanese
Korean
Mandarin
Mediterranean Europe
Covers Albanian, Greek, Italian, Macedonian, Maltese, Serbian & Croatian and Slovene.

Nepali
Pidgin
Pilipino
Quechua
Russian
Scandinavian Europe
Covers Danish, Finnish, Icelandic, Norwegian and Swedish.
Spanish (Latin American)
Sri Lanka
Swahili
Thai
Thai Hill Tribes
Tibet
Turkish
Vietnamese
Western Europe
Useful words and phrases in Basque, Catalan, Dutch, French, German, Irish, Portugese and Spanish (Castilian).

Lonely Planet Audio Packs

The best way to learn a language is to hear it spoken in context. Set within a dramatic narrative, with local music and local speakers, is a wide range of words and phrases for the independent traveller – to help you talk to people you meet, make your way around more easily, and enjoy your stay.

Each pack includes a phrasebook and CD or cassette, and comes in an attractive, useful cloth bag. These bags are made by local community groups, using traditional methods.

Forthcoming Language Survival Kits
Greek, the USA (American English and dialects, Native American languages and Hawaiian), Baltic States (Estonian, Latvian and Lithuanian), Lao, Mongolian, Bengali, Sinhalese, Hebrew, Ukrainian

Forthcoming Audio Packs
Indonesian, Japanese, Thai, Vietnamese, Mandarin, Cantonese

LONELY PLANET PUBLICATIONS
Australia: PO Box 617, Hawthorn, Victoria 3122
USA: 155 Filbert Street, Suite 251, Oakland CA 94607
UK: 10 Barley Mow Passage, Chiswick, London W4 4PH
France: 71 bis, rue du Cardinal Lemoine – 75005 Paris

PLANET TALK

Lonely Planet's FREE quarterly newsletter

We love hearing from you and think you'd like to hear from us.

When...*is the right time to see reindeer in Finland?*
Where...*can you hear the best palm-wine music in Ghana?*
How...*do you get from Asunción to Areguá by steam train?*
What...*should you leave behind to avoid hassles with customs in Iran?*

*For the answer to these and
many other questions read
PLANET TALK.*

Every issue is packed with up-to-date travel news and advice including:

* *a letter from Lonely Planet founders Tony and Maureen Wheeler*
* *travel diary from a Lonely Planet author - find out what it's really like
  out on the road*
* *feature article on an important and topical travel issue*
* *a selection of recent letters from our readers*
* *the latest travel news from all over the world*
* *details on Lonely Planet's new and forthcoming releases*

To join our mailing list contact any Lonely Planet office.

LONELY PLANET PUBLICATIONS
Australia: PO Box 617, Hawthorn, Victoria 3122 (tel: 03-819 1877)
USA: 155 Filbert Street, Suite 251, Oakland, CA 94607 (tel: 510-893 8555)
UK: 10 Barley Mow Passage, Chiswick, London W4 4PH (tel: 0181-742 3161)
FRANCE: 71 bis, rue du Cardinal Lemoine – 75005 Paris (tel: 1-46 34 00 58)

Also available Lonely Planet T-Shirts. 100% heavy weight cotton (S, M, L, XL)